GREGORY WOODS was born in Eg[...]
began his teaching career at the U[...]
Nottingham Trent University, whe[...]
and Lesbian Studies in 1998. His w[...] in the
United Kingdom. He was awarded a [...]sity of East Anglia
in 1983, and a DLitt in 2006. In ad[...] his poetry collections, all
published by Carcanet Press, he is also the author of a number of critical
books, including *Articulate Flesh: Male Homo-eroticism and Modern Poetry*
(1987) and *A History of Gay Literature: The Male Tradition* (1998), both
from Yale University Press. He has been a member of the board of directors
of East Midlands Arts and is a Fellow of the English Association.

Also by Gregory Woods from Carcanet Press

We Have the Melon
May I Say Nothing
The District Commissioner's Dreams

GREGORY WOODS

Quidnunc

CARCANET

LEEDS LIBRARIES AND INFORMATION SERVICES	
LD38486881	
HJ	10/01/2008
821.9	£9.95
S035179	

First published in Great Britain in 2007 by
Carcanet Press Limited
Alliance House
Cross Street
Manchester M2 7AQ

Copyright © Gregory Woods 2007

The right of Gregory Woods to be identified as the author of this work
has been asserted by him in accordance with the
Copyright, Designs and Patents Act of 1988
All rights reserved

A CIP catalogue record for this book is available from the British Library
ISBN 978 1 85754 946 1

The publisher acknowledges financial assistance from Arts Council England

Typeset by XL Publishing Services, Tiverton
Printed and bound in England by SRP Ltd, Exeter

Contents

Civilisation	7
The Cistern Sings	8
A Triumph	9
This Fastness	10
Heroic Memoir	12
Consuming Love	13
Against Perfection	14
Due Process	16
Instruction	17
Quidnunc	18
Fiction	23
Canon Law	24
Descent	25
Report Back	26
Design or Accident	27
Cablegram	37
Budleigh Beach	38
Those Years	39
Heart of Cold	40
Autumn Sessional	41
Man on Train	42
How to Belong	42
Queer Pedagogies	43
The Newstead Fandango	46
Days of 1912	56
Proust's Way	56
One for the Master	57
My Zealotry	58
Sir Osbert's Complaint	59
Negotiate Salvation	71
My Sprig of Lilac	72

Acknowledgements

Earlier versions of some of the poems in this book have appeared in *Anon*, *Gay and Lesbian Review Worldwide*, *Launderette*, *Magma*, *PN Review* and *Take Five* 05 (Shoestring Press). 'Sir Osbert's Complaint' was originally commissioned by the East Midlands Literature Officers' Network as part of the *24/8* project in support of the region's writers. Drafts of some poems were commented on by friends and colleagues, including Catherine Byron, Tina Jay, John Lucas, Clare MacDonald Shaw, Mahendra Solanki and Diana Syder.

Civilisation

We tilled a land ungenerous with its
resources, barely scratching at the surface

for its reluctant benison. Between
its gaunt, eroded outcrops we conserved

a topsoil dry and sparse but capable
of nurturing our basic needs, the corn

our staple and the grapes and olives we
eventually produced enough of to

engage in trade with strangers from the north.
Our fishermen brought home with them new words

as well as fish, and trinkets for the children.
We decorated the clay pots our wine

and olive oil were stored in with ornate
designs passed down from hand to hand without

superfluous inventiveness. The beauty
our girls were famous for we hid indoors,

protected from the sun and foreign lusts.
The beauty of the boys we put to use:

their blithe physiques inspired us both in bed
and on the battlefield. We sent them out

to show the enemy, then shipped them home
in body bags. The keening of the women

was proof we lived in a heroic age.
With manly sympathy, we harnessed them

to the demands of population growth.
Another season brings another crop.

The Cistern Sings

The cistern had an echo of its own,
a diffident acoustic you could pipe
a string quartet into – the space was large
enough to hold one, deep enough to lose
one in – prepared to echo anything
the nervous airwaves shivered into it.

On the day I killed my neighbour
                I was late for lunch.
The children had already like
                a plague of locusts
left a famine at the table.
                I sent my sister
to the neighbours' for the rations
                they'd abandoned when
I spoke to them an hour before.
                The screaming women
hardly noticed her among them,
                hungrier than they.

History happens in
domestic spaces. Pots get broken.
The parade ground is
deserted, the uniforms
empty on their hooks.
In lieu of gossip, now the time has come,
                the machete, the hound.

A Triumph

As if a hand had turned the volume down
the shouting stopped. A last command, conveyed

around the bay by bugle taps, called off
a push no longer needed. Victory

surprised them, even though their lives had had
no other purpose since they left the cradle.

While some unsheathed their swords
from corpses, others stopped the steel in mid-

assault as if commanded by a sculptor
to hold the pose. A handful of last lives

were spared by arms already flexed to end them.
These lucky ones were saved for slavery.

The lads were knackered, too exhausted to
have anything to say or much to think.

They pitched their lances in the sloping sand
like beach umbrellas. Gagged by hero-worship,

the water-boys came round with goatskin bags
and sympathetic looks to take the edge off

the unforgiving love and loss of comrades.
Each breastplate, peeled aside, revealed a breast

more human, therefore more divine. Mere leather
could never capture such a plain effect,

no matter how adept the armourer.
They left their sandals beached like landing craft,

their helmets empty at the water's edge
like the discarded shells of hermit crabs.

They scoured themselves with black volcanic sand
then slept along the beach like tourists, packed

as close as space demands to take the sun
before the evening's bleak debauchery.

This Fastness

That happened. Now it's over. The remains
Lie rusting in wet grass. Historians
Will leave the subject in the archives to

Mature. No point in rushing out posterity's
Opinions on ourselves until the line
To be adopted is agreed. Was this
The triumph that the victors claim or the
Disaster of the other faction's version?

The press divided as their barons chose,
Along conventional political
Defiles. The so-called public never knew
The facts of the affair, but only the
Romance. They swallowed what their spoons conveyed.

When darkness fell the televisions rose.
So wisdom was received. The past had been
Forgotten for us and remembered in

The whisper of an airbrush. Soldiers sat
In mufti on strategic streets, alert
In unmarked cars. A single order could
Have summoned reinforcements instantly.
At least the State was still in working order.

The precious freedom of the individual
Was never compromised by lack of will
Or funding. Liberty is paramount.

To every lock we have a key – and turn
It. Every law has get-out clauses. All
The rights that anyone could ever want
Were won so long ago there's no need now
To think of them. It's all in place. Complete.

Of happiness there's no need for pursuit.
Policemen smile on routine duties and
They help old ladies cross the hostile street.

That couldn't happen in whatever place
This isn't, overseas and far away,
Where garlic-eaters speak those spicy tongues
And kiss each other on both cheeks for no
Apparent reason. Bloody foreigners.

Heroic Memoir

The day I joined the army
                they declared a war.
I thought of it as mine.
                The crowds at the station,
the bunting, the band,
were there for me,
                the women, the kisses,
                the handshakes, the men,
were all for me
                and me alone.
They flew me overseas.
I parachuted through a fog
                into an island jungle
set apart for heroism –
                not heroism in the abstract:
mine. And mine alone.
Mosquitoes bred in HQ's labs
                appeared to have a taste
for only one man's blood.
So did the enemy.
My comrades died defending me.
                And when the truce was signed
with Quink in Sheaffer pens
                by fops who never once
set foot outside
                expropriated country houses
from which the war was run,
the truce was worded in the very way
                you might have recognised
as no one's tone of voice but mine.

Consuming Love

Damon and Pythias, lovers renowned
Beyond their native Syracuse, astound

The cynics with the strength of their devotion.
Exchange of fluids, more a magic potion

Than mere biology, sustains their passion.
Each shares with the other his precious ration

Of manhood. Short of Ichor, there's no liquor
More apt to toast a union. Semen's thicker

Than blood. Their love ferments inside each other's
Digestive tracts, making them more than brothers.

Against Perfection

1

Much as a virgin's shyness
Is more secure than sureness,
To any sum a minus
Comes as an added bonus.

2

The losers beat the gainers
When cheated of the honours
Conferred on lazy runners
Who won by cutting corners.

3

The element of fairness
Needs burning in a furnace
To be restored to rawness.
The ox respects its harness.

4

Aeneas swaps the blueness
Of Dido's gulf of Tunis
For consciousness's anus,
The cistern at Avernus.

5

Perfection is a menace.
The Erichtheon's cornice,
The Liebestod of Linus,
A pair of Nike trainers…

6

A life of gourmet dinners
(Yes! we have no bananas),
No other face as soon as
You fall for Valentino's…

7

Bing Crosby, king of crooners,
Blue Riband ocean liners,
Of all the Bach B minor's
Delights its countertenors…

8

Anonymous as pennies,
A flawless diamond's miners,
Siena's urban planners,
The Taj Mahal's designers…

9

As sturdy as lianas,
The look of Tarzan's sinews,
Of comforts marijuana's
Or, failing that, Nirvana's…

10

What expert piano tuners
Accomplish with their spanners,
The boys you meet in saunas
Who can't conceal their boners…

11

The Virgin Mary's cleanness,
An English valley's greenness,
At Wimbledon the tennis,
Of Errol Flynn the penis…

12

The motion of Adonis
Between the thighs of Venus,
The bridge of sighs at Venice…
Perfection is a menace.

13

(By contrast, misdemeanours,
Mere lapses of good manners
Or good taste by lesser sinners,
Are treated as if heinous.)

14 Envoi

As fatherly as Cronus,
The mother of all diners

(His hide as thick as rhinos',
Undaunted by harpooners,
Gaunt Eroses on schooners),

The whale subsumes the highness
And dryness of its Jonas
With peristaltic slowness,

As slow as any *annus
Horribilis* is. FINIS

Due Process

The prophecies were wrong. Translation had corrupted
The scriptures. Bedlam! All the barbershops erupted
With loud recriminations and I-told-you-so's.
Some walked out unshaven. A draughts match came to blows.

Those who had waited in the mountains for the rain
Of fire returned to their apartments. Inhumane
Expressions were contorting even pretty lips:
For no one can abide a late Apocalypse.

When prophets fail the most effective thing to do
Is find a scapegoat. Though it makes no difference who
Gets picked, he has to be thought evil, not a martyr –
Beyond the pale, *persona non* cocksucking *grata*!

Instruction

This is how you brand a man.
Most of it is obvious.
You hold him down, a boot across the neck will do,
but check his breathing
in the dust beneath his face.
You rip the clothing off him with a knife
or cut the toughest bits
and worry the rest between your teeth.
Let his only anaesthetic
be humiliation –
he will thank you for real pain,
a single incoherent chant of gratitude.
Remember to take food.
We find men smell of barbecue.
They make us salivate.
I once went down between the olive groves
from where the ruined lighthouse makes its mark
to wash my sandals at the water's edge.
I saw a boy there, resting on the rocks,
who had the kind of body you could train
for an atrocity.
He offered me a portion of his lunch,
the better portion, all the better to
beguile me by.

Quidnunc

1 *A Suitable Expression*

Remembering himself
a tasty little number
the grandest prefect could
come crawling to and beg
for favours, he perfects
the tying of the tie,
the brushing of the hair
and the adoption of
a suitable expression.
Though little visible
remains of who he was,
at heart he's still the same
manipulative tart
who always used to get
if not what he desired
what other boys would envy.
He knew from the beginning
that market value knows
no absolute: a thing
is worth what you can get
for it; you pay a man
as little as it takes.
The wife he sees into
the limousine is loved
for qualities she brings
to the appearance of
a life beyond the boardroom.
She means as much to him
as any personal
assistant, even if
the fact that she can't be
so easily replaced
keeps him awake at night.
He needs his sycophants
as they need him, and yet
with every oily word
the more familiar than
the one before through sheer
predictability,

how can mere compliments
assuage the emptiness
of such superiority?
If only one of them
could flatter him as once
Maltravers Senior did,
hot from the rugby pitch
and desperate, transformed
into a truffling pig.

2 *Out of Uniform*

The hero brandishes
his handlebar moustache
at any pretty thing
that happens into his
peripheral awareness.
He stands as tall and straight
when at his ease as on
parade, and dresses for
the dullest day as if
for Sergeant Major Chubb,
since having had to trust
his life to whom no man
has ever feared another.
The sensitivity
with which his senses sense
phenomena beyond
the capabilities
the rest of us are blessed with
has stood him in good stead
in times of conflict as
in those like these of peace.
And yet there comes a time
in even such a man's
undeviating march
towards the charnel house
when chance delivers change
and certainty is shot
to pieces. Something in
the press of people heading
for the delirium
of yet another waltz

reminds him of his batman's
expressive face, alert
with rustic irony,
projected on a shockwave
into a reflex of
his wing-three-quarter hands.
He tells himself to pull
himself together, but
while part of him complies
his better self rebels.
A shudder of self-doubt
and just as Jenny Barton
(coincidentally)
comes into view, he ducks!

3 *What Now?*

What now? Whatever next?
Patrolling his estate,
the fields and brakes a line
of ancestors had worked
for centuries to pass
from hand to hand to him,
Blyth cast his eye along
old boundaries inscribed
as proof of ownership
in parish records dating
from before the Conquest.
The very hedgerows bore
if not his name the mark
of his inheritance.
And yet, when all is said,
he'd sell the lot to build
a garden suburb on
if other fates were promised
by other circumstances.
Turning for home he called
the dog to heel and hitched
his trousers up as if
to ready them for some
uncertain purpose hatched,
alas, before he'd been
subjected to the first

exacting flurry of
his season of regret.
He'd taught himself that love
is not a necessary
condition of existence
or even happiness.
He'd learned to live alone
(unless you count a pug
for company) and spread
his tranquil sleep across
a prairie of a bed.
Hot water bottle and
a box of tissues were
sufficient substitute
for a compliant wife.
The market would provide
an heir, his lack of faith
enough of Paradise
to last as long as ashes.

4 *Lady van der Meer's Win*

She bided what was left
of what was once her time
with one eye on the clock,
the other on that less
than nothing, lower than
the belly of a snake,
her lifelong enemy
the Duchess of Deceit.
Not till the stroke of twelve,
and then not till the twelfth
had played its echo out
around the gilded dome,
did Lady van der Meer
let slip the chance remark
rehearsing which had kept
her out of circulation
and out of harm for weeks.
So long indeed had she
been gone that there were those
who hardly recognised her
but by the rubies at

her throat and the revenge
implicit in her glare.
The husband at her side
was barely visible,
his small-talk audible
only to those for whom
the insignificant
holds weight: diplomacy,
the game of empire, the
sad likelihood of war...
The rest had but to wait
and curiosity
would be rewarded with
whatever came to pass –
defeat or victory.
In the event – for an
event it was – the wit
of one was parried by
the other with a smirk,
as if a duchess could
by dint of blood alone
shrug off the paramount
necessity of face.
A pin was heard to drop,
a curl came loose, and we
self-consciously went back
to Monsieur Vaudet's pudding,
that miracle of sweetness
half tamed by bitterness.

Fiction

I borrowed a novel
from a man who recommended it,
hoping he would see
I'd all the qualities a man like him
might look for in a friend.
The book was written in a turgid voice –
letters to the hero from the heroine and back,
with no stylistic difference between the two.

I gave it back and praised it.
Not a word of truth.
              He liked to hear me lying.
              By accident
I happened to achieve my aim. His friendship,
              his esteem.
A little dab of irony behind the ears.

There would be nights in the heat of summer or
the blast of winter when we couldn't sleep
and I would beg the man
              to read to me.
He read the letters from the lover to his mistress.

As if to obviate the problem,
one style for two protagonists,
we did without her letters back.

We grew to love suggestive silences.

Canon Law

The temple has remained in use
for fifty generations. The hinges at the gate
have been replaced and gone again
more times than any mortal can recall.
The steps are so worn down
they almost satisfy the latest regulations
on wheelchair access. Faith, too,
has suffered its refinements, certain facets
worn away but others redefined
for new conditions. Regulations
writ in stone – the tablets in
the gilded shrine – on vellum and
passed down from priest to priest
and family to family are still
regarded with respect if not obeyed.
The younger generations shock the older
as they once shocked their own;
the old seem to the young
incapable of ever having overstepped the mark.
Pigeons nest around the buttresses.
Incomprehension overcome by mere experience –
what better system could creation have devised
for making sure
the man who shields his eyes to read
the writing on the wall
– graffiti marking teenage stomping grounds –
stays rooted to the spot,
to all appearances a martyr turned to stone,
although symbolic little more appreciated in
the rush hour than a paltry ornament?

Descent

The bald peak reveals nothing. You could begin your descent
In any direction. There is no path to speak of. But
Hardly have you gone down to a point where your head is
Lower than the mountain's pate than the uneven rocks force
Your feet into its own chosen channels and you find a
Path. At first it is wide enough only for one foot at
A time, so that not only are you descending at a
Perilous angle, nearer the vertical
Than the horizontal, but you are having to balance
As if on a tightrope; and not only that, but the path
Generates its own avalanches of scree under your
Boots, threatening to send you down the mountain on your arse.
At the first fork in the path a decision confronts you,
Important enough in itself but not worth a delay
In your progress, given that this is only the first of
Many forks, demanding the first of many decisions.
Even the time it takes to toss a coin would be too long.
Just keep going: for the path you choose will have its own fork,
The next path another, the next another, and so on,
All the way down into the green foothills, where the gradient
Will be kinder to your aching calves, the softer surface,
For long stretches cushioned with thick moss, will spare the soles of
Your feet the worst effects the upper slopes set in progress,
The blisters you seem to be developing already,
Judging by the fact that you've started limping slightly,
And each new path will be a little wider than the one
Before, a little more inviting, sweeter on the eye
As well as the legs, a positive joy to walk along.
Even without time to look at the view, you'll look at it.
Before long you'll be sauntering down grassy bridleways
Through woodland and waving at complete strangers in sandals.
When you get onto paved lanes you'll find the crossroads have been
Helpfully signposted, even to the superfluous
Extent of reminding you how far you have come and where
You started from: the name of the mountain will loom large in
Your retrospect without distracting you from the need to
Find your way. There will be people to ask, and once your road
Is broad enough to appear on it, a map to consult.
You could have brought a compass, you could refer to the sun,
Or you could rely on your own instincts, such as they are;

But in the end the slope and the highway will be your guide.
You'll find yourself walking down the central reservation
Of a motorway, between the crash barriers, kicking
Discarded bottles and cans, deafened by traffic noise, choked
By fumes, with nowhere to turn to, inches from sudden death.

Report Back

We wrote on his body
To teach him a lesson.
When the message is bloody
The nerve-endings listen.

We caught his attention
With precision of scansion.

One is not taken lightly
When the audience bleeds.
He listened politely
To the point of our blades.

Oh yes, did I mention
We caught his attention
With rope under tension?
Man's greatest invention:
Erasing men's future
With methods of torture.

The throat in which he jabbered
His confession of treachery
We adapted as the scabbard
To the thrust of our lechery.

Let the palate of the zealot
Taste the bullet in his gullet.

Design or Accident

1 *Sainthood*

At the sickbed of the saint
                we prayed for his immortal soul
as if it needed it.
                His eyes were bloodshot.
He could hardly see us
                let alone have named us –
he must have thought us
                either total strangers
or family so close as not to need reminding of.
Perhaps his last emotion
                was embarrassment.
                God rest that soul.
The nun who nursed him also slept with him,
                judged by her demeanour.
She knew his wishes
                before he forbore to express them
with that corpulent, raw tongue.
                (He'd been tormenting
his sensuality with glasspaper.)
                Virtue was impressive.
We brought it grapes and roses
                and listened to its death rattle
with all the concentration of
                a schoolboy on a sermon.
Don't take the name of God in vain,
                don't touch yourself,
above all
don't put money on
                the matter of morality.
No matter how well you behave, you can't win.

2 *The Way Things Change*

A puff of smoke in the hills
among the half-built second homes.
The delayed rumble.

War looks so small.
Even the shortages in the market

can be explained away:
a rush on the good cuts of meat before the weekend,
congestion at customs
in the port.

When friends fail to return
say
they went abroad –
a new life in America,
a job opportunity he couldn't turn down.

Even the bombers
in formation, heading east,
droning through the night,
might just as well be carrying
the young men we miss
and their heartbroken girlfriends
on package holidays.
A week or two
of sunburn and late night raves,
tripping over foreign phrases,
picking at suspicious foreign food.

3 *Ways of Surviving*

And another thing.
All the men are leading double lives
     so perfectly researched, equipped and executed
         they believe them both,
incapable of seeing
     this one contradicts the other.
All the women doubt them, doubt them both.
The situation has become ridiculous.
         The strain of keeping up
     appearances has
generated nervous tics: a shiver
     at the corner of one eye,
        a twitch, a twinge, a shudder.
Survivors of atrocious wars have often suffered less;
     at least their womenfolk
         gave them the benefit.
And another thing,
     before I go. Remember this.

You change your costume, adopt an accent,
even learn alternative constructions of the past.
You weep when angry, smile when pained.
You stretch out on the other body,
                not the one desired,
                    and whisper the expected script.
It doesn't matter. Human nature will survive.
                What won't
is not to be predicted.
Men sleep like babies
                and wake up in tears,
                        soiling themselves,
                              begging for the nipple.

4 *Rightness*

Did you feel a twinge?
I am that muscle,
the one that gets pulled
and sends a pain up the leg
like a boy at the door
with the worst telegram you can imagine
so that the athlete
has to pull up short
halfway down the back straight
and falls to the ground
clutching his calf or his groin.
His scream another telegram.
The commentator mentions me,
I have a history,
how sad it is my trouble has recurred
at this of all times
when there might have been a medal and
a bunch of flowers.
He mentions me again,
I'm being packed in ice.
I'm being talked about
and packed in ice,
which is as much as I could have expected.
There's a logic to these things,
a sense of rightness.
One thing leads to another
without warning

and everyone says it's not fair
it's not fair it's not fair.
It all slips into place
as if somebody planned the whole thing,
though nobody did. Nobody did
as far as I know,
not even me.
Just before you screamed
I took myself by surprise.

5 *Our Mouths to Meet*

The white man is sitting – in a cane chair in a tropical
garden, a beer within his reach – in what he thinks of as
solitude (perhaps he even sees himself in 'splendid
isolation') when, peering more closely into the shadows

of some especially fleshy, large-leafed greenery, he
suddenly sees white eyes in a black face peering back at him;
or faces plural. It is not that he imagined he was
completely alone – someone must have served the beer, after all –

but that the others (or the Others) should be there but not
sentient. The shock is in seeing himself seen. Apart
from the fact that this makes him a matter of interest –
even if the eyes appear indifferent – and therefore that

some kind of performance is expected of him (which makes him,
in his stiffness, self-conscious), more importantly the presence
in the greenery (the Bush, the Jungle, the Darkness) stakes
a prior claim. While he is only surrounded by silent

slaves and flunkies, as little seen as possible, like the
servants in a great house who have their own narrow corridors
and even staircases concealed between the walls so that
they vanish and appear with that greatest of servile graces

'the utmost discretion', he is the unquestioned master
of all he surveys, and therefore need not question his own
mastery; but as soon as he is watched he is under
attack. After the resentful glance, there will surely come spears.

The eyes in the undergrowth are a man's or a woman's,
whichever the white man fears the more. As soon as he is watched
he has to ask himself what is being seen – and instantly
he knows that the other does not see him as he sees himself.

6 *Matter for Debate*

This idea
                that passion is the highest good
needs digesting with a pinch
             of paprika.
Let passion kill the man next door
               and send its squadrons of the poor
across the river into the enemy regime.
Let boys come home in body bags,
              their unspent promise dry
in shrivelled purses.
     This idea
               that passion, of all things,
      the clench and bloom of it,
the selfishness, the selflessness,
deserves to be revered – an icon in
         each bedroom drawer
              and outside cinemas –
to the extent of faith
         is stated in all languages
         in loud environments
     by anyone
with anyone to listen. Tongue and lips
were shaped to state such matters,
      intellect was not.
The boy in the library
      face in a book
          licks a finger
            to turn the page.
    He looks up
    between one sentence and the next.

7 *Laying Siege*

These are the books he reads,
great ramparts piled against the visitor
in ruins here where hordes have forced their way
but still formidable
along the border most in need
of his defending. Given good binoculars
you'd get a distant purchase
on whatever titles hadn't faded from the spines.
Authors' names were pseudonyms, without exception –
hardly worth the effort taken to decipher them.
The reader, to besiege him, you have to find
in any one of any number of locations,
in each a chair and reading lamp, an ashtray
and an empty glass. He moves at night
from place to place, his profile low
but aquiline – to judge by the portraits of
ancestral genes, the oils that hang
wherever he is never found.
You half expect, if you'd just send the drummer boy
down to the pantry for a shaving from the leg of lamb
the lad would stumble over him:
the reader, bookless, on a stool
in total darkness, listening to something scratchy
on his iPod, polite when interrupted
but fiercely protective of his victuals.
The boy returns, a little out of breath,
attempting to put into words
the reader's resolute refusal to say anything.

8 *Our Moralities*

We sat around the scrubbed-down table
                debating our moralities:
should any human being worthy of the name,
                the species *Homo sapiens*,
do this or that for reasons such as these and those?

Yes, we said with gravid gravity, or no,
                each according to his taste.
One tamped the dead tobacco in his pipe,
                one jingled the small change
in a trouser pocket, one kept clearing his throat.

                    We loved each other because
we loved impressing each other. These were friendships
                which would last a lifetime.

                A siren interrupted us,
climbing from the port, laborious from hairpin to hairpin.
                We closed the shutters
and turned down the lamp. It guttered and went out.

Nothing we had said in our discussion
                had any resonance. A rifle butt
enforces silence when it hits a door. A man of action in
a uniform reduces other men
to this paralysis:
huddled in each other's arms, hardly daring to breathe,
rattled by each other's heartbeats.

9 *Detail*

There were others around us, even others between us,
others in our thoughts. But when others saw us in the street,
or thought they understood what they had overheard us say,
they thought of us as indivisible, the perfect couple.
It's likely they imagined what we did between the sheets.
On summer nights they smelt the sweat of our exertions
throughout the city; asthmatics were advised to stay indoors;
the pillows of children were rendered dreamless with cologne.

Did I love you? Do I still? We might as well believe it,
for who are we to doubt the word of witnesses
so certain, so many, so at one? If I consult my memory,
somewhere between the one who came before, and the more earthy one,
the kid who liked it dirty and dressed accordingly,
successor to your fabled age, I lock on detail:

you always laughed before you came, and yawned
the moment after, but liked to silence me with flesh.
I saved the things I couldn't say for later. Even now
they spring to mind like fresh ideas. I love you, darling,
God, I love you, don't stop now, do it again, I'll never leave you.

10 *Being Shadowed*

They watched us from the ridges as we passed,
suburban redskins with an eye
for signs of weakness, apt to pick on the
unfittest for survival.
We kept together, strength
in numbers, fellowship in self-defence,
and kept a steady pace along
the river bed.
They called across us as the sun
went down, long yearning notes
you might have thought a wolverine
might make when wounded
and abandoned by the pack,
a dialogue of solitudes from peak to peak.
Shuddering, we huddled closer,
arms around each other's shoulders.
Someone tried to start a song
but gave it up when no one joined him.

No longer silhouetted on the sky
and silent now
they didn't let us think they'd gone.
You could just make out when they inhaled
the points of cigarettes
and even think you smelt the smoke,
convincingly enough and unconvincingly enough
to spark a vague suspicion.
I imagined it. There's no one there.

11 *In Time*

Salvation came in dribs and drabs,
the piecemeal prize for abject lassitude,
a lump of sugar for the gelding
that never lived up to the pace,
and then another lump.
Don't spare the horse's teeth.
                                        Peaches in the gutter.
Why did the knocking at the door begin
the moment we put out the light?
Once we had decided who should go,
why, when you got there, did it stop?

Who but a stranger at the wrong address
                              could it have been?
The summer is wasting itself, nothing gets done.

We said our prayers and sent our thank you letters,
raised our hats, held open doors,
swallowed before we spoke,
forbore to scrape our chairs across the tiles.
Our parents would be proud of us.
Our courtesy we offered to the world
as what it looked like to be civilised:
from stone to iron to bronze to steel to silicon –
the obsessive collection of manners
                              making man.

But what we did,
                            we rose above ourselves,
                            we pardoned each other.
Amusing ourselves, erecting pyramids.

12 *Great Architect*

I designed a building. Then
                        another, larger.
      Then a cluster,
outlandish shapes united by curved walkways.
      My medium was concrete,
                      reinforced, of course, with steel.
I loved its wan immensity,
      the glare of it in sunlight,
                  the dirty grey when wet.
My practice took on brilliant young apprentices,
      those earnest boys with cold grey eyes
                    and steel-rimmed spectacles.
      We were commissioned to design
            whole cities.
I obliterated landscapes with the free sweep
            of my pen.
            It was assumed
      I did so with a merry heart,
but nothing could be further from the truth.
Each forest felled, each river dammed,
      all noxious marshland drained,

                    bore down on me,
            their weight transmitted through my spine
            and sturdy femurs
                        to the solid ground,
            but I was never crushed.
Correct equations underpinned my most flamboyant whim.
In time, although the corners of the concrete
            crumbled, and rust stains from the steel
                        disfigured my great walls,
I grew to love the shanty towns
            the people lived in
                        in the shadows of my spires.

Cablegram

Am bleeding. Send bandages
with all despatch. Have been
reduced to bitter tears.

Morale of men uncompromised,
all rumours conclusively denied.
Cat's whisker permanently tuned
to popular frequency,
Woodbine ration undiminished,
natives friendly to extent
of sycophancy: tug forelocks,
stand aside if in the way,
affect to be convertible
by men with giveaway Bibles.

All well to that extent but me.

We await the invention of mechanical
miracles: above all a Land Rover
to take the weight off our blisters.
But in the meantime Coca-Cola
and antibiotics would do. More than do.

If some of us become delirious (I mean if I)
you will be in receipt of cock-
eyed messages. Do not ignore. Repeat.
Do not ignore. Imperative
you try to understand. Draft in interpreters,
dragnet the universities.
Pressgang the sensitive.
Threaten blackmail if need be.
Believe me, sirs, need will.

Budleigh Beach

Contempt for natural verses
Prevented my thinking of
This as other than mere space, as
Fit to laze in as to leave,

Where a once mannerly river
Is teased by too spare a cleft
Between beach and cliff to fever
Pitch and tumbles the sea's shift

For quick access. Water finds
Water. But the hills we scalp
For harvest and what sky blends
Its distance with the bay help

Nature turn imagination
To account. The sea reflects
And contains colour. Illusion
Is close enough to the facts

To be convincing. This clouds
Confirm by zincing the surf
Even as the river bleeds
Clay on it. No disbelief

Can deny beneath the coursing
Sky this red and silver storm
Of setting sea – truth reversing
Nature, *contra naturam*.

In mid-air an upturned hull,
Rung by the breakers, alarms
The coastguard, while like a whale
His green helicopter swims

For its life. To this device
I consult the mouth as clue,
Just as to look into space
We must focus on a plough.

Those Years

In those years, which he would remember as being
perpetually rainy, he envied the normal,
        the carriers of

umbrellas, the walkers of doggies. He tried to
imagine having a hobby to fill the hours
        between work and sleep

but couldn't imagine what that hobby might be.
When he entered a crowd, palming himself into
        their midst with uneasy

glances in all directions as if slipping a
counterfeit coin into a full purse and drawing
        attention to his

dishonesty, he couldn't help noticing the
expressions of involvement on so many of
        their faces, the look

that says, or claims, I am a part of you all, one
among many, not apart from you all, not that
        at all. He saw how

they held their umbrellas over their doggies to
protect them from the incessant rain, soldiering on
        to whatever their

expected destinations, looking forward to
whatever their expected interactions with
        whichever colleagues,

friends or relatives they would encounter, never
for a single moment lapsing into despair
        or boredom, because

they knew that if the worst possible thing happened
they could always end a heavy day by folding
        the umbrella and

    drying off the doggy's paws with an old rag
before spending the whole evening with their hobby,
        then going to bed;

whereas he, at that time in his life, had only
to look at a little doggy and it would be
        yapping at him and

nipping his ankles like a land-bound piranha,
and the moment he ever raised an umbrella
        it turned inside-out

in an unforeseen gust, yanking his arms almost
out of their sockets and tugging him into the
        puddle he deserved.

Heart of Cold

Whatever else there is to say about him, the besotted,
Among whom I include myself, were never near to sated,
Although we got our money's worth. Extreme detachment suited
Both him and us. We wouldn't have been nearly as excited
If anything unphysical had ever been inserted.

No part of him has not been fondled, worshipped, kissed or licked
By strangers. Every inch of him has been not only looked
At but assessed by touch and taste, concavities unlocked,
Convexities enfolded, nothing merely rather liked
But fallen for, obsessed about, providing what they lacked.

His eyes are empty as a statue's, and his heart as hard
As marble. Yet for all their threat his muscles, lightly haired
And honey-tanned, desired and envied by the common herd,
Provide him with his income: any portion's to be hired
For any purpose. Beauty never stored a richer hoard.

Autumn Sessional

Did you and I never finish that conversation,
The one in which circumlocution and avoidance
Made a pact, broken only for moments of peevish
Honesty or, out of nowhere, pure fabrication,
With the apparent intention of foiling any
Risk we might run – God forbid – of communicating?

The leaves were on the turn, reddening at the edges,
But a north wind was whipping through the old sash windows,
The whole house rattling as if it were being carted
Over some Oregon-like trail by the unsettled,
And the central heating had switched itself off, leaving
Us prematurely Novemberish in September.

Would it have been better if I had reached out, even
Without actually touching your face, as I wanted
To, but at least signalling with one limpid gesture
That there was something in all the things we weren't saying
That couldn't in any case be said, or would giving
In to that impulse have seemed like a childish short-cut?

By November itself September was already
A pleasant and all-too-distant memory, misting
Into all the other events semi-remembered
And only dimly brought to mind when excavated
From the crushed strata of errors that go together
To reveal the history of a life unfinished.

Could I with this, this tentative display of fussy
Organisation, add a few finishing touches
To that conversation across the kitchen table
Over half-empty coffee mugs, or would a poem
Just add to the distance, too crafted, even crafty,
To say anything to the point, anything helpful?

When you had gone I lay alone on that wide mattress
You know so well, that raft adrift on the slow whirlpool
Of the adventure you took part in or abandoned
At will, which suited us both, and I masturbated,
Huddled under the duvet, imagining nothing
So solid as your stringily muscular body.

Man on Train

When I establish eye contact I find
    The glaze of his indifference daunting:
He's glaring at me and his glare is blind.
    I want him but he finds me wanting.

How to Belong

Behave as if they know you here.
Use gestures and expressions of a kind
conveying a relaxed familiarity
with where things are and how things happen.

Laugh at any dog that barks at you
as if to say, Why there you are again,
my friend, and here I am again!
(But carry poison for emergencies.)

Never stand perplexed at any crossroads,
never peer enquiringly into a doorway's darkness,
never use the interrogative
unless to an imperative effect.

The world is full of strangers who
might just as well be friends or enemies.
Imagine everything about them you don't know
is like the distance between lovers, impenetrable fog.

Queer Pedagogies

for Alan Sinfield

I've crept away for an early supper from the
Queer Studies conference and made my way across
        Waterloo Bridge without
    noticing the view, still spitting feathers,

incensed by the complacent turd at the session
on 'queer pedagogies' who wittered about his
        students as 'ignorant
    amateurs' taking part in 'a drama

they don't know they're in'. No wonder this bastard gets
the negative student feedback he's complaining
        so huffily about,
    implicitly fingering the lot of

them as homophobes, the gay ones no less than the
rest. Amateurs they may be, and ignorant to
        boot, but they seem to have
    got the measure of this professional.

Having safely crossed the Strand at the traffic lights
I slip into a lighter daydream, sweet nothings
        on the tattooed boy from
    San Francisco who wrapped his arms around

himself while shyly speaking the language of high
theory as trippingly as if he were just
        spinning some good-natured
    gossip about an absent special friend.

Waiting for my meal, I'm distracted from Vasko
Popa's *Collected Poems* by a prosaic
        drama only one of
    its participants knows he's in, although

it's clear he wants to attract the attention of
another: the waiter has taken a shine to
              the pretty blond boy who's
       brought his even prettier blonde girlfriend

for an early dinner before the theatre.
Busy as he is, in a hurry from table
              to table, or between
       the kitchen and the customer, he keeps

making detours to the couple, offering them
more to eat or drink before they've finished what's on
              the table in front of
       them, addressing his attentiveness to

the boy but having to accept the politely
dismissive replies of an unfortunate fate
              in the shape of the girl.
       He's stockier, darker, more muscular

than the object of his pressing need, but about
the same age, nineteen or so. I can imagine,
              as the waiter does, the
       two of their bodies in conjunction like

an auspicious alignment of planets, pale and
smooth alongside darker and hairier, the one
              opposed to the other,
       their disparities in perfect balance.

But the same smile the waiter bestows on me for
the joyful moment when he delivers my meal
              the boy has ignored or
       simply overlooked, again and again,

immune to its undoubted glamour in the face
of his girlfriend's composure, and by the time they
              get up to leave, that smile
       has changed into a disappointed pout

     – if only the silly kid would just notice it –
more seductive still. Life goes on, of course, and so
               does waiting, so that by
     the time he brings me my coffee, my waiter

has cheered up and is chattering away as if
in that brief season of obsession he really
               had the boy, held beauty
     in his hands and shaped a memory so

detailed and precise as not to need preserving;
or else, so busy, so happy, so open to
               the possibilities
     of a lifetime, he'd simply

forgotten the existence of that lovely youth.
Back in my hotel, I imagine Socrates,
               the day's discussions done,
     lowering himself wearily on to

the desolate narrowness of his pallet, and
sighing: Those boys, those boys! They're pretty enough and
               all that, but when it comes
     down to it, such ignorant amateurs.

The Newstead Fandango

If a writer should be quite consistent
How could he possibly show things existent?

Byron, *Don Juan*

1 *Oxen of the Sun*

Vile insect, dear reader – whichever you prefer – the writer
Salutes your willingness to waste your time, an eager martyr
Upon the altar of my Muse, by reading me when greater

If not more thrilling penmen can be found in any gutter.
(How touching the false modesty of genius!) The later
It gets, the more inclined you are to idle, and the fatter

You grow, the more you need a voice like mine. While readers loiter,
I spring across their vision with the sleekness of a cheetah,
Providing them with heroes, while that paragon von Goethe

Is churning out potboilers like *The Sorrows of Young Werther*,
That sissified sub-Sisyphus who thinks of nothing better
Than hauling his emotions up a slope – obsessive rotter! –

Before releasing them again, and ditto, ditto, ditto...
As an impassioned suitor he's as flaccid as he's neuter.
If that's the kind of thing I'm up against I'll give no quarter.

2 *The Wandering Rocks*

A hot September afternoon, a roasting field of barley,
Largesse in such abundance, all the world seems touchy-feely,
And even the most misanthropic farmer waxes jolly.

The Earth is manifest in such variety, it daily
Demands to be acknowledged with an attitude part holy,
Part blasphemous. We owe a duty to esteem it highly

But estimate its future under Man's control but poorly –
Ill-chosen habitat for such a self-destructive bully.
While Satan was condemned to surf the landscape on his belly,

Man stands aloof from it, perhaps remarking in its silly
Quiescence his disruptiveness. Could he but fly he'd duly
Remove himself from gravity with levity and sully

The very breeze with his inconsequence... A steeple's hourly
Reminder of mortality rings out across the valley
And fools with time to kill accuse the clock of being early.

3 *Nestor*

In literature, preserve us from the pleasant and the subtle.
There's not a single English poet whom I wouldn't throttle
In the attempt to shape his feeble voice to something brutal –

Just as I'd rather struggle than relax in matters coital.
It's news to me if life is long enough to waste on little
Particulars. You have to act as if it would be fatal

To sacrifice contingency to comfort. Never settle
For anything predictable. Let every moment startle
With its capriciousness. The man who vegetates in foetal

Suspension looks to me as if he thinks himself immortal.
With every year I add to life's accumulated total
I feel compelled to greater energy, because it's vital

If not to conquer life at least to know you fought the battle.
So, far from slackening, I have in mind, as down I hurtle
Towards oblivion, to press my club-foot to the throttle!

4 *Lotos-Eaters*

Accumulate a fortune! Live forever! Win the Derby!
Would anything you wished for, drunk, be worth the having, sober?
Who but a chump would choose to live as long as Colley Cibber

But write as badly? Must there not be more to life than jabber
And less than mere longevity? In every living fibre
Of my physique I yearn for not the product but the labour.

If writing verse were like a conversation with one's barber,
And sonnets could be left as structureless as an amoeba,
It might be possible without much thought to shape a flabby

Excuse for prosody. But poetry is not a hobby;
Still less, reliable as compost for the money-grubber.
Deprive me of that will to write and maybe I, just maybe,

I could endure a lifetime nibbling lotoses on Djerba –
Or lettuces, at least. Far rather that than fill my abbey
With supererogatory detritus bought on eBay.

5 *Sirens*

I'd swear an oath on all the Torahs, Granths, Korans and Bibles
A plague of theists can devise, that no affray of Babel's
Was louder than the countryside an English poet troubles.

Wherever oak matures, a pasture slopes and water burbles,
The warbler, faithful to its onomastic fortune, warbles
Among the reeds, and bream play hard to spot above green pebbles,

Some twerp, mistaking flatulence for inspiration, dabbles
In poetry, the easy art of self-expression, foibles
Like goitres on display for all to see. He walks, he scribbles –

But knowing nothing of the Nature he applauds he cobbles
Together paperscapes of views he thinks his verse ennobles.
Where once the voiceless woods were resonant with peals of bluebells,

His rhyming seems to satirise the silence it enfeebles.
He keeps returning to the slopes on which he lost his marbles:
Parnassus is a hill in England, wild with elk and shoebills.

6 *Aeolus*

I've had a dream of storm and shipwreck that's recurred with leaden
Predictability since I was someone called George Gordon.
I wish I could, if only once, wake up in leafy Arden,

But Fate dictates that I should be disturbed in bed by sudden
And overwhelming surges, whirlwinds, deluges, unbidden
By any Prospero but somnolence of mind. My wooden

Four-poster sloop would founder were it not so lightly laden,
Provisioned for the night and crewed by one stray lad or hoyden.
(If these are shells that were their ears, why must the thunder louden?)

Since 'no man dies from love but on the stage' (John Dryden),
It may be we must die for other things: some 'other Eden',
Perhaps, or an adventure the success of which would gladden

The disenfranchised and the disenchanted. Short of Snowdon,
These islands boast no higher principle than to unburden
By effort of philanthropy the lot of the downtrodden.

7 *Calypso*

Marooned upon a distant shore – or so I dreamt – I brooded
On Fate's impersonal vindictiveness. As heavy-lidded
As coffins, my believing eyes had opened on a shaded

And bosky beach, a paradise – but no! for down the wooded
Embankment came a regiment of redcoats, muskets loaded
And poniards drawn, and I was led away, on all sides guarded

Against the impulse of escape. They took me, bound and bloodied,
To where they forced me to abase myself before their bearded
Infanta, she who had to be if not obeyed avoided.

Without the power but what a vicious temper stung her powdered
Attendants into wielding with their quirts, she barely nodded
And I was whipped within a whisker of my wits. I pleaded

With her in vain: for I was working off, with interest added,
The ransom that she made it clear I couldn't have afforded.
I woke at noon. My heart was broken and my loins ungirded.

8 *Cyclops*

Since the originality of Adam's sin, disorder
Has been humanity's accustomed element. I shudder
To think of how routine must shrink a man. Could Henry Tudor

Have founded his adulterers' religion as a plodder
Down given paths, or Good Queen Bess have scuppered the Armada
By sticking to a feminine regime of paste and powder?

Without the least ambition as a virgin or beheader,
Although I wouldn't sell my soul but to the highest bidder,
My body's going cheap: he never flourishes in purdah.

For all that it was outmanoeuvred by the bloodless Buddha,
Desire is an implacable but lenient invader,
Impatient as the geisha in the shade of the pagoda

Or adolescent psychopaths who murder for al-Qaeda,
That, once surrendered to, releases you. What could be madder
Than to expect stability between the swan and Leda?

9 *Lestrygonians*

When I consider how my night is spent, from sunset's dimming,
Through hours of rakish company and profligate consuming,
To the oblivion of morning – when, by blindly squirming

Across the bed, I ascertain with whom (or what) my coming
Was hammered out – I'm often moved to set my mind to rhyming,
Inspired to art by what the killjoys spend their spare time damning.

For all that I'm a placid chap, some folk deserve a bombing:
So rich is life, I keep encountering do-gooders, scheming
To save an unrepentant soul from lechery and gaming,

As if by souring all my pleasures they'll escape their looming
Apocalypse. So say I'm sick, I'm dead, and send them, foaming
And moaning at the mouth, to blazes. Let the God they're hymning,

Should He see fit, get off His arse and do His own condemning.
If Byron spends unwisely, who the Devil is he harming?
Humanity will fold before His Lordship starts conforming.

10 *Scylla and Charybdis*

Forgive me if I write as if reporting to the chairman,
Or spouting prejudices to impress a stoic barman,
But there are times when not to rant you'd have to be inhuman.

For Christianity to thrive, must every prayer or sermon
Be simplified to satisfy the dumbest catechumen,
Or should the Mysteries be left for wonder to illumine?

In literature, the plot is all that matters to the layman,
But that's just superficial detail – was it Piers Plowman
Who met a pie man, going to the fair? – to any Brahmin.

Technique, in verse no less than in seduction, needs a showman:
So I deploy the most uncommon language I can summon,
As flashy as the church at Vierzehnheiligen by Neumann,

To leaven the familiar thing. Hyperbole's a hormone
That, blended with the bloodstream of the most impassive woman,
Will undermine her modesty and, in due course, her hymen.

11 *Circe*

The truth is simple. What you have to do to win a lady –
From flattering her Mummy in the manner of a toady
To making conversation with her dullard of a Daddy,

Who by a constant rule must be, at best, a fuddy-duddy –
Is apt to leave you unenthusiastic, dull and moody.
And when at last you reach the daughter she becomes a bloody

Beguine, her pious drone unchanging as a hurdy-gurdy:
Suburban, earnest, churchy, turgid, surly, worthy, wordy...
Whereas a boy arrives equipped with nothing but his body,

Forever primed with neat testosterone, alert and rowdy,
His appetite unmitigated by a conscience, seedy
As pomegranate, the precise embodiment of bawdy

– His mind is like his body: dirty, flexible and hardy –
And leaves you, by the time you've finished, feeling spent and giddy.
Yet, when the hurly-burly's done, he's still erect and ready!

12 *Nausicaa*

The worse for wine again, if none the worse for that, I staggered
Down the dawning corridor, bouncing off the walls, as haggard
In every mirror – they were legion – as a guilty niggard

Tormented by a conscience for the poorer men he'd beggared,
And as I went I called the name of Robert Rushton, sluggard
(Yet still abed, my lad?), erotic as the verse he triggered.

You'd be impressed at how, despite the alcohol, I swaggered
At not unstoppable but decent speed, a randy blackguard
With one thing on his mind – anticipating which, I sniggered

And sprung a stiffy. Sleeping and undressed (well, I'll be jiggered!),
I found him on the camp bed in my dressing room. He augured
Those pleasures even greater than the sight of him. I figured

As I aroused him with my antic hands and he, beleaguered,
Attempted to escape, the pill I'd give him could be sugared.
So take my purse, says I – then I'll be fleeced but you'll be buggered.

13 *Proteus*

What I delight in is a shameless lad who'll drop his breeches
As nonchalantly and as often as his wretched aitches,
And yet when crossed adopt the airs and graces of a duchess:

If nothing else, his chutzpah should be mentioned in dispatches.
But, just as much, I love a boy who suffers the reproaches
Of all the gods if what he covets he so much as touches.

I'll cleave to him while he's asleep and taste his twitching flitches,
Then wake him into lechery with kisses sharp as leeches...
(The veil discretion draws is soon awash with pearly splotches.)

I'll watch him, hushed but flushed still, pouting as he slouches
Away along the corridor, the hypocrite, self-righteous
In his repudiation of our pastoral debauches

– Until the next time! I could fill a thousand parish churches
With victims of delicious guilt, and not run out of letches.
Ashamed desires repeat themselves, like trusty pocket watches.

14 *Telemachus*

I had a reputation on the playing fields of Harrow
For making an advantage of what should have caused me sorrow.
When bullied for my foot or complimented as a fairy,

I never let it pass but gave a master-class in fury –
For whence but from a schoolboy's ardour lead the paths of glory?
Renowned not only for a temper but a heart as fiery

As Strómboli, I started to be figured for a hero,
Diminutive but worth the courting. I was never surer
Of love than in that season of aggression, never nearer

Reciprocating kiss for kiss, devouree for devourer.
While every boy in my embrace became a doe-eyed houri,
My pallet vied with the divans of Isfahan and Cairo.

This tongue was never hindered by so much as a caesura:
Each friend elicited a flood of love, like Petrarch's Laura,
Until his moment passed and Mother Nature made him hairy.

15 *Eumaeus*

It comes again: the image of a beach – West Indian, Grecian,
Or Polynesian – refuge from a freshly stealthy ocean.
I'd dance my retinue along it, Bacchus done by Titian,

Awake to any brief encounter, whether with some Persian
Enchantress, spicy Chinaman, or rough and tufty Russian.
I'd even, given a convenient slab of shade and cushion,

Delay my course to pow-wow with a viridescent Martian.
There's no man in the world with whom I wouldn't hold a session,
So long as brain or manhood weren't unduly Lilliputian.

But in the end I'd seek a friend, more mellow and Confucian,
Enough of a philosopher to make some sense of passion,
Who'd recognise me from my work, if not as his relation,

As one in search of equanimity beyond confusion.
With luck, should Fate not stint on sheer contingency, emotion
And reason could combine to undermine the last illusion.

16 *Penelope*

The seasons keep themselves amused by taking turns unknotting
Each other's handiwork, as if to make the perfect setting
The Dissolution made these ruins for. Instead of shutting

Them down, I've put them up for sale: the time has come for parting.
For why go wandering abroad and keep the old girl waiting,
When someone else could buy the place and give it a more fitting

Attention? Which is worse, neglect or openly deserting
The neighbourhood for good? I'd go no more a-roving (quoting
Myself) if life were nearer being over bar the shouting,

And if the house were not so much in need of less mistreating:
I colonised one corner and reserved the rest for sporting
Activities, the hall for battledore and target shooting,

The cloister and the stairs for all the noble arts of fighting.
Yet nobody who ever lived here could have been more doting,
For all the boot and stirrup marks we made around the skirting.

17 *Hades*

When circumstances play against me and the cards are parlous,
When even on a diet of boiled fish and veg the molars
Play up, a mistress who believes she owns me waxes jealous,

The villains I imagined were my friends turn into spoilers,
And life itself descends into the mire, my usual solace
Is to unleash my pen against said felons, whores and dealers.

But in the end, no matter how divinely penned and lawless
My lines, the sword is mightier than the pen. However fearless,
A poet's heart availeth naught unless he nail his colours

To freedom's mast. And so, a scourge to torturers and jailers –
Like Samson a deliverer, if not, God willing, eyeless –
I'll promise finer fare to both my stomach and my phallus,

Prepare myself for intercourse with foreigners and sailors,
Get Hobhouse to provide the cundums, shuck my winter woolies,
And venture south to bring about the liberty of Hellas.

18 *Ithaca*

To Greece, then, and to freedom – for if better men have quested
More vital grails, I haven't heard of them. I've never jousted
With windmills. The ideals to whose regalia I'll have mustered

The ordnance of my pen and person, nothing has outlasted.
And afterwards, when all the feasts have been profusely feasted…
The tallest of my tales been told and all my boasts been boasted…

The last of my forbidden lusts been well and truly lusted…
Should it transpire, unlikely though it sounds, my time's been wasted,
I'll reconcile myself to the petard with which I'm hoisted.

Arriving home, my spirit, like my feet, forlorn and blistered,
The lake iced over and the window-panes ornately frosted,
I'll summon Rushton to deliver gin and extra worsted

– My valet will be company enough, the lucky bastard –
And settle down to a routine less tranquil than sequestered,
Renewing my acquaintance with the solitude of Newstead.

19 *Ulysses*

Perhaps by then, when I come home, I'll find the abbey dirty
From spread of industry and with the wealth of nations smutty,
From its foundations to its pinnacles, beneath a sooty

Empyrean. I'll ail to find myself, though hale and hearty,
Surrounded by the merchant classes, freshly hoity-toity
With ownership of men, and inappropriately matey.

I'm picturing myself the other, lesser side of forty,
Developing a paunch, receding, maybe even gouty,
But putting in an effort, face-hair trimmed into a goatee

Or mutton-chops, distinguished looking, if perhaps no beauty,
Awake to how the pretty like a gentleman who's witty.
I'll have returned triumphant, fêted on all sides by totty,

Revivified, and scattering my semen like confetti...
So never mind how are the mighty fallen: I'm so natty
You might as well declare, with awe, how are the fallen mighty!

Days of 1912

Outside, the bedlam of the human race
Proceeds. The silence in this book-lined space

Is metaphorical, conveyed by tone.
Aloft, aloof, not lonely but alone,

The poet listens, then rejoins the noise
To look for gods disguised as mortal boys.

So human are these heart-convulsing few,
Each is a miracle. Descended to

The common herd but from more lofty stock,
They raise the spirits as they stir the cock.

Proust's Way

I've dignified a house of ill repute
With mother's furniture. The surly brute

Who runs the place does so from mother's chair.
The men who come to work there brush their hair

With mother's brushes, backed with tortoiseshell.
Within this heavenly faubourg of hell

My mother's son's at liberty to clutch
The parts his mother told him not to touch.

His virile heroes flex their pecs and lats,
And while he masturbates they torture rats.

One for the Master

In clauses so subordinate they grovel
To distant and aloof main verbs, my novel

Attempts to fascinate the feckless young
With written language's prosthetic tongue;

But even its most tantalising grammar
Is too dull to distract them from a glamour

More aphrodisiac by far than these
Parentheses within parentheses.

There is a purpose to such Chinese boxes:
They keep one safe from love and other poxes.

My Zealotry

What the devil did you think?
                 – a flock of goldfinches
       like a beaded net
       fishing for berries among the shrubs.
What did you expect to see, a whale?
Sit down at the table by the view.
           Keep your mouth shut.
Write your blessed love letter –
                much good may it do you.

See, the mountain is spouting its ash.
You'll find it on your counterpane
when the cops come knocking at dawn.
         At best, you'll sneeze.

Why did you wait so long, so many months,
to fly down here? We were waiting,
          every one of us,
                 each with a phrase of tepid welcome.
Did you think we would fall to our knees?

Here in the garden, cushioned in soft dust,
I abase myself, naked.
I eat the dust, I fuck it, I wet it.
                Give me no instruction, lord –

I know your answers. I bind my eyes.

Sir Osbert's Complaint

for Catherine Byron

Part One

1

When a thousand coal-gas crocuses ignite like pilot lights
In the grass between the tree trunks, and the scented air excites
Both the senses and the intellect, we long for shorter nights.

2

By the time they've flickered out the air is warmer by degrees
And, depressing though the drizzle is, at least it doesn't freeze.
There's a feeling of renewal on the saturated breeze.

3

Sure enough, the afternoons become reluctant to give way
To the moment when our nanny calls us children in from play
And we dawdle by the door before relinquishing the day.

4

Not that play was what we did when out of sight and out of mind.
If a child had the effrontery to ask us, we declined.
Given books instead of playthings, we were not the playing kind.

5

The society our parents kept we mimicked in our own:
Their jejune, dogmatic arguments; that hyperbolic tone;
And the scenes we'd seen two adults act without a chaperone.

6

But our parodies were arid: we forgot to be amused.
The lampoon and the reality were hopelessly confused.
We became the very adults we'd complacently abused.

Part Two

7

A new century came in. The motorcar replaced the horse.
Every bath we took was heated by the coal mine at its source.
(The industrial's the only revolution I endorse.)

8
Oily rainbows on the fishpond, flaky cinders on the lake,
Claggy slagheaps on the skyline and domestics on the take –
Yet there's nothing in Arcadia that our gardens couldn't fake.

9
At a distance from reality the hedges lead the eye
Into Italy or ancient Greece beneath a leaden sky,
With a fountain or a temple to identify them by.

10
Though our daffodils are hardly more Italian than the Swedes,
Cultivating them is more a deed of habit than Candide's.
What would make it more Italianate would be a clump of weeds.

11
Every vista has a gist, a sort of statement of a creed,
Unbelievable in beauty but in logic guaranteed
To attract one to the factor to which all perspectives lead.

12
Never accurate, the sun dial is a wiser judge of time
Than the most acute chronometer's mechanic pantomime.
Tempus fugit says enough, obscured by moss and hardened slime.

Part Three

13
Conversational location shaped the content of our talk.
Disagreements were concluded by a choice where footpaths fork,
The direction of our thoughts by the direction of the walk.

14
It was easy to escape whatever choking atmosphere
Was reducing them to silence in the adult stratosphere:
Any path or passageway could make an infant disappear.

15
Mother Nature, as we knew her, had an organising mettle,
Like a nanny. Telling stories to enthral us, she would settle
Our anxieties with posies. We knew nothing of the nettle.

16

I was not so much a bookworm as a bookish sort of leech,
Draining books of every corpuscle of what they had to teach.
(I had heard the mermen singing, in my daydreams, each to each.)

17

I remember with relief a play I wrote while still a child:
Not a word did it contain but what I stole from Oscar Wilde.
It was torn up by my sister, whose good taste it had defiled.

18

Though precocious as a reader, as a writer I was slow.
Masquerading as an author, I mistook the easy flow
Of my nib for wit, parading everything I didn't know.

Part Four

19

With the loyalty a Boyar feels for sullen Mother Russia,
One attempts to save one's ancestry from time's remorseless crusher.
What the Sitwells feel for Renishaw, the Ushers felt for Usher.

20

When a home's been in your family this long, you feel related
To each godforsaken stone. And that's the very thing I hated:
Like my brother it was haunted, like my sister crenellated.

21

It's the typical estate: a country house in formal grounds,
Rambling woods, a lake to boat on, open fields to ride to hounds,
A view beyond to wooded hillsides, the horizon out of bounds.

22

Like the dynasty it serves, rough-hewn by long vicissitude,
Irrespective of the point from which its oddity is viewed,
The aesthetic of the building is by any standard crude.

23

Where you might expect a doorway, there's a brutal chimneystack,
Like a boxer's broken nose on which you dare not turn your back.
Yet the building seems defensive as if tensed for an attack.

24

Horizontal, squat, as grey as Sheffield's weather, this façade
Serves as backdrop to the lives we act out under the regard
Of the statues on the lawn, our audience and bodyguard.

Part Five

25

What with Sachy holding back, and what with Edith holding forth,
With yours truly in the middle, holding little of much worth,
We established all the habits that would mark our time on Earth.

26

We enjoyed ourselves, though sober in the thrust of our hilarity:
For such purpose as we had was to abolish a disparity
By donating Sitwell brilliance to the national culture's charity.

27

Our modernity was earnest. We conducted an impassioned
Celebration of the new – but we preferred our newness rationed.
Though mere novelty wears off, you can rely on the old-fashioned.

28

In the country we conducted our concerns by candlelight
Well into the nineteen-fifties, and kept faith with anthracite.
Reading verse through megaphones would hardly put the past to flight.

29

What we managed as a trio we could not have done apart.
We were thought of as a single beast, a Cerberus of art,
Whose three contrapuntal voices represented just one heart.

30

All for one and one for all!... I was distracted from this course
By a fourth, one David Horner. Our affair involved, perforce,
Being granted from my siblings an emotional divorce.

Part Six

31
There's a way love has of catching one completely unawares,
As if organised by Providence to herd us into pairs,
With no leisure in our pleasure to make sense of our affairs.

32
We reject discrimination as if throwing off our cares
And commit ourselves to Eros's imaginative snares,
Too enchanted by a hairstyle to have time for splitting hairs.

33
It's a platitude: the smaller things are bigger than the bigger.
I met David. He seemed civilised, and vigorous in figure.
If romance requires an instrument, his silk tie was its trigger.

34
I was always the pursuer, he was always the pursued.
Like a virgin pleading modesty, he forged my servitude
With reluctance so convincing I was utterly subdued.

35
In the manner of the ancients, he became my other half.
Though it might have been expected that we'd kill the fatted calf,
We discreetly shared a bottle, a bread pudding and a laugh.

36
Being often seen together, we were treated as a pair.
No one asked the question no one answered: colleague, friend, affair?
In the end, we dared to share a *pied-à-terre* in Carlyle Square.

Part Seven

37
If one quails at being crushed beneath an omnibus, or coshed,
In their denser concentrations one avoids the great unwashed.
From a height they look like insects. How one prays they could be squashed!

38
With society sclerotic and the culture half asleep,
Nothing changes for the better, nothing moves but at a creep.
It would take a leopard shepherd to direct this herd of sheep.

39
Mussolini had the right idea to save a nation's pride.
I had hopes that Oswald Mosley could, colossus-like, bestride
What was left of Merrie England, but my optimism died.

40
When the Blackshirts came to Renishaw they started with a march
From their charabancs along the drive and through the gothic arch,
But the stiffness of their uniforms proved little more than starch.

41
We retreated to the house for the duration of the war,
But despite the country setting we weren't spared the bombers' roar.
They were aiming at poor Sheffield, but just missing Renishaw.

42
What kept us there together, more the bloodline than the heart,
Was fidelity to family and passion for our art –
Plus the fact we had our rooms a hundred yards or so apart.

Part Eight

43
In the orchard, Edith overcomes the words with which she grapples
And records her peerless triumph on the page the sunlight dapples.
If the worse comes to the worst, the shadows comfort her with apples.

44
When it comes to deeds of derring-do, some talk of Alexander.
But Hephaestion is left till adulation turns to slander.
I remember both when David is demobbed, a Wing Commander.

45
The returning hero hurries to discard his uniform,
Like Odysseus in the bedroom in the calm after the storm,
All the more the welcome husband for his relapse to the norm.

46
These two people I love most seem never quite on speaking terms:
To discuss the weather with them is to stir a can of worms,
And mere greetings pass between them like a frank exchange of germs.

47
Rhododendron bushes guard the English like defensive banks,
As intimidating as the sand dunes hiding Rommel's tanks,
But they flower in an hour like a fusillade of blanks.

48
In a deckchair on the terrace in the sunshine, David dozes.
When you try to think, your mind goes pink with the scent of bloated roses.
What mankind proposes, God ignores; and matter decomposes.

Part Nine

49
Unexpectedly one sees one's seen the last of the wisteria.
From now on the shadows lengthen and the flowerbeds are drearier.
The high season is succeeded by its lachrymose inferior.

50
Irretrievable, time passes. Things get worse. The waistline thickens.
Was it God who made us kneel to *hoi polloi*, or was it Dickens?
Clement Attlee did the dirty work whose legacy still sickens.

51
In their element, all metals tarnish, oxidise or rust.
Carpe diem, if you must, but don't blame me if uncurbed lust
Leaves you feeling life's worth living, an illusion you can't trust.

52
Waking early, I can hear the garden boy is raking leaves.
I can picture how his muscles play below his rolled-up sleeves.
No physique was better fitted to light gardening since Eve's.

53
Though he's bulky as a boxer, his self-consciousness is louche,
And his sulkiness is lovable, less thuggish than farouche.
How unmissable to kiss his – what's the word for it? – his *bouche*!

54
If I dress and hurry down I'll find no Corydon, but just
Dead leaves scudding through the doorway on a cold, autumnal gust.
Golden lads and girls all must, like carpet-sweepers, come to dust.

Part Ten

55
If the levellers had time while they reduced the Welfare State
To its lowest common multiple, they might anticipate
What the absence of the beautiful would leave us with, but hate.

56
They prefer one to have castles in not Italy but Spain,
Built with fantasies and figments, like a segment of Cockaigne,
So that nobody should benefit from beauty's rich demesne.

57
What has art to do with anything, or anything that matters,
If, instead of hitching beauty to the truth, it merely flatters
Ideologies – an enema for dormice and mad hatters?

58
One's life follows its own sequence, like a living alphabet,
In which brandy follows port, a hacking cough a cigarette,
Spelling out its narrative, and never sidetracked or upset.

59
When a writer's philosophical – I am, therefore I think –
He distends his cogitations with incontinence of ink,
As if nothing could suppress him but a bullet or a shrink.

60
Freud has probably identified some syndrome of the pen,
A neurosis in which childhood reasserts its hold on men.
Diagnosis is straightforward, but the cure beyond our ken.

Part Eleven

61
Since a night when I was sleepless and some presence slapped my cheek
I've been reconciled to dying. The revenges they might wreak
Keep the spirits fit and active in their games of hide and seek.

62
Planning hauntings of his enemies beguiles an old man's time:
I shall lurk behind the arras like a witness to some crime,
Taunting Philistines and critics in the fashion of my prime.

63

When I'm dead I'll have no deadline but untold eternities.
Without feet I'll creak the floorboards, without hands I'll jangle keys.
When I go is up to God, if not to Parkinson's Disease.

64

The old sawmill by the lake looks like a grounded man o' war
In the helicopter flicker of the shedding sycamore
While I wander, humming Walton, through the woods at Renishaw.

65

As a boy I gathered conkers here and carried them indoors,
Looking after them as if they were the eggs of chests of drawers.
I imagined I could hatch antiques to rival Renishaw's.

66

Like the hero of the epic, I found trouble at my door.
I'd come home for some repose, but quoth the haven: Nevermore.
There were more than ghosts to haunt me in the halls of Renishaw.

Part Twelve

67

Could that tapping of a finger on the glass be Peter Quint,
Or an agitated, leafless branch delivering a hint
Of the Reaper's urgency, enough to crack a heart of flint?

68

Could that rustle in the passage, like a paper carnivore,
Or like a present being wrapped, be someone wrapping at my door?
Could I be becoming nervous of the sounds of Renishaw?

69

Could that tapping at the window or the rustle in the corner
Be material expressions, from the living building's fauna,
Of unease – the moths and dormice, getting bored with David Horner?

70

There are times when love is war, however long the corridor.
I had nowhere to escape to. When you're cloistered with a bore
Life's a prison. Nowhere's big enough, not even Renishaw.

71

Make the most of what you've got. The rest's for God to reimburse.
One could do a great deal worse to mitigate old age's curse
Than attach oneself to someone who can double as a nurse.

72

Love's no less a form of ownership with equal than with chattel.
I employed a man my most abusive tantrums failed to rattle.
The result was a romance with which I fought a losing battle.

Part Thirteen

73

What did David's love amount to but a relic from the past?
As ephemeral as summer, it was never meant to last.
It's enough that we had years together nothing else surpassed.

74

When I've pointed out some trinket in the hope he'll be impressed,
I've been comforted to hold him at a distance, yet distressed
To discover that my lover is now just another guest.

75

If I see him in the bathroom, greying hairs on flabby chest,
I dissociate him from the golden boy I once caressed;
I can hardly recognise this stranger, shaving in his vest.

76

Once, his absences upset me; now, his presence just depressed.
The solution was for him to leave. ('It might be for the best.')
Let him sacrifice himself: for *dulce et decorum est*.

77

It was now I chose to choose between the past and future tenses
By exchanging David Horner for my new amanuensis
And, in some eyes, taking leave of both my homeland and my senses.

78

Since I shied away from telling him myself, I went one better
And instructed my solicitor to do it in a letter:
Sir, my client is dismissing you as his onlie begetter.

Part Fourteen

79

I'm tempted to pre-empt the dusk. The indoor status quo
Is asserted with drawn curtains, blocking out the heavens' glow.
Either Sheffield's lit its streetlights or it's coming on to snow.

80

By the dawn the middle lawn is like a bridal featherbed.
On the yews we use to limit it, a dimity's been spread,
Like a dust-sheet over furniture when everyone has fled.

81

Nothing stains the linen's virtue but the footprints of a fox
And the silence makes it whiter like the stopping of the clocks
Or the vague, intrusive presence of an absent chatterbox.

82

But by nightfall it's been sleeting and the snow's begun to melt,
The bridal bed's been covered with a blanket of grey felt.
Not that spring is yet upon us; but one wintry spell is spelt.

83

If the breeze is from the east you can make out the M1's cars,
For the isle is full of noises, and the slightest zephyr mars
What it ventilates. The very welkin tarnishes the stars.

84

The austerity of breeding is a burden I've passed on
To my brother, whom posterity relies on for a son.
Where the first-born yields, the second has a first-born of his own.

85

As my father did before me, I'd decided to withdraw
To a warmer garden's scenery on terraces galore.
To the English, I left England; to my nephew, Renishaw.

Part Fifteen

86

Give me peace and beauty, peace and beauty, silence with a view;
And a man without opinions to explain the beauty to.
Or, failing that, there's Proust: *À la recherche du temps perdu*.

87

If the Muses had allowed me to alleviate the pain
Of nostalgic longing for a time I'd rather not regain,
I might have said: Last night I dreamt I went to Renishaw again.

88

But, in truth, I've had my fill of it, as it has had of me.
It takes more than bricks and mortar to support a threnody.
If I dream of anything, these days, it's of mortality.

89

I was not the kind of man who always wondered what things meant.
It sufficed that they existed for me, whether Heaven-sent
Or the product of Contingency, that dapper malcontent.

90

I keep asking my own conscience if I ever used my eyes
To do more than seek one falsehood in a lethal pack of lies,
Seeing nothing of the truth throughout a life of compromise.

91

I imagine I've a badge in one of Heaven's pending trays,
Saying: Sceptical believer with a decent turn of phrase.
That's the best that I can hope for when the last trump duly plays.

92

What endures? A thousand pages of my memoirs. Little more.
Edith's poems, at a pinch. And Sachy's offspring. Little more.
And the Sitwell seat at Renishaw. There's this and little more.

Negotiate Salvation

Who is it? What do you want?
Sir, you stand here at my door,
hat in hand, demanding
more than you should want, far more than I
could dream of delivering.
Your whiskers are frozen, a fretsaw of ice.

Sir, I could offer you less than you ask:
the house itself, my wife and daughter,
the Alfa in the garage.
For what return?

You smile. Has nobody denied you?
So clench your fists for me, sweet master,
patient on my threshold,
while I make my peace with apathy.
Never disappoint your sons. Carry out
the threats you least intended in
the first place. Mine
the pasture for your vengeful team.

What you want, sir, what
your needs dictate
               the two of us can find –
not here, not there –

between us,
in this space
where breathing can be seen.

My Sprig of Lilac

I woke without misgivings and had breakfast in the garden,
Surprised by silence. In these happy doldrums, nothing sudden,

A breeze made sluggish canvas of the paper I was reading.
My lilac tree was on the turn, its brief abundance fading,

A few intrepid bees collecting what they could before
Its modest pyrotechnics sputtered out for one more year.

I hadn't mown the lawn for weeks, and strapping dandelions
Had staked their meagre claims, an unassuming crowd of peons

Who might impress the painter of a battle with their candour
But not his snobbish patron. Powerless, should someone blunder,

As someone always does, the rank and file exert their numbers
Against impossible opponents, termites chewing timbers

A splinter at a time, their ethos of self-sacrificial
Commitment to the body politic completely social,

Yet not enough to make a single one of them a hero.
By some unconscious mechanism guarding me from sorrow,

I must have missed this item several times: the paper said
Thom Gunn is dead. Without a moment's pause, I understood

That that would be the morning's problem – trying to imagine
A life without new poems from the master, as a virgin

Might wonder, darting furtive glances at a brawny, burnished
Physique, what happens once you've drunk the mirage and it's vanished.

I listened to my tinnitus, but heard Ecclesiastes:
Oh, vanity of vanities! No more divine than dust is,

Humanity makes do with being better than what howls
And bolts its meat uncooked; but whether animals have souls

Is not the point so much as if they have a sense of humour.
Our silliness is what preserves us from the earnest drama

Of Nature. Even solved, no theological dilemma
Is more substantial than an echo in the house of rumour.

While we down here are moithering in pointless sadness,
He's chatting up the Seraphim. It's cool, it is, this deadness.